SHOUTS AT SUNRISE

2006-7 NMI
MISSION EDUCATION RESOURCES

❊ ❊ ❊

BOOKS

EIGHT STEPS FROM THE EDGE OF HELL
From Addiction to Ministry in Ukraine
by Sherry Pinson

EVERY FULL-MOON NIGHT
Life Lessons from Missionary Kids
by Dean Nelson

GLIMPSES OF GRACE
Mission Stories from Bolivia
by Randy Bynum

THE POWER OF ONE
Compassion as a Lifestyle
by Ellen Decker

SHOULD I KISS OR SHAKE HANDS?
Surviving in Another Culture
by Pat Stockett Johnston

SHOUTS AT SUNRISE
The Abduction and Rescue of Don Cox
by Keith Schwanz

❊ ❊ ❊

ADULT MISSION EDUCATION RESOURCE BOOK

MISSION FAMILIES
Editors: Wes Eby and Rosanne Bolerjack

SHOUTS AT SUNRISE

THE ABDUCTION AND RESCUE OF DON COX

KEITH SCHWANZ

Nazarene Publishing House
Kansas City, Missouri

Copyright 2006
by Nazarene Publishing House

ISBN 083-412-2375

Printed in the United States of America

Editor: Wes Eby
Cover Design: Brandon Hill

10 9 8 7 6 5 4 3 2 1

DEDICATION

This book is dedicated to everyone who regularly prays for the safety of missionaries and missionary kids.

As the video camera recorded his arrival at Chicago's O'Hare airport on Christmas day 1995, Don Cox stated, "My biggest Christmas gift is to be alive at this moment. And I thank the church so much for their prayers." Starting to weep, he quickly added, "Oh, thank the Lord! Thank the Lord! Thank you, church!"

The Cox family, December 2003. *(L. to r., front)* **Phil and Matt;** *(back)* **Paul, Cheryl, Don, and Mike**

CONTENTS

Dr. Keith Schwanz is an ordained elder in the Church of the Nazarene and has served as a pastor, professor, and writer.

A freelance writer, he is the author of *Words of Life and Love: World Mission Literature Ministries,* an NMI missions book for 2004-2005 NMI, as well as other books and numerous articles in *Holiness Today, Herald of Holiness, Illustrated Bible Life,* and *The Preacher's Magazine.* He served as editor of *Sainteté à l'Éternel!: chants pour le peuple de Dieu* (Holiness Unto the Lord: Songs for the People of God), the first French hymnal produced by the Church of the Nazarene.

Keith is the adjunct professor of church music at Nazarene Theological Seminary where he directs the Seminary Singers and is the chapel coordinator in addition to his teaching responsibilities. He serves on the NMI Council of the Olathe (Kansas) College Church of the Nazarene.

Keith is married to Dr. Judi Schwanz, professor of pastoral care and counseling at Nazarene Theological Seminary. Together they have taught in pastors' retreats and conferences in Mexico, the Dominican Republic, Puerto Rico, Canada, and the United States. They live in Overland Park, Kansas, and have two adult children, Karla and Jason, and one grandchild, Judah James.

PREFACE

I first heard Don and Cheryl Cox tell this story while on a Work and Witness trip to Guadalajara, Mexico. I heard it a second time at a Christmas banquet a couple of years later. When asked if I would put the story in written form, I eagerly welcomed the invitation. This is a great story of God's sustaining grace.

Don and Cheryl had many conversations with my wife and me throughout the writing process, often during a shared meal. Each time more of the story came to the surface. We could talk for weeks, and I'm convinced additional details would emerge during each conversation.

The format of NMI missions books governed the decisions concerning what to include in this volume. Every author faces the sometimes difficult decision to leave some things unstated. Even in writing the gospel, John acknowledged that Jesus performed many miracles He could not squeeze into the account (see John 20:30).

Human drama rather than hostage negotiation methodology drives this telling of the story. I deliberately avoided anything that might give criminals an advantage should they seek to harm another missionary. This account describes the responses of faith in an extremely difficult situation. I tried to craft a compelling story so the reader would *feel* the despair and *know* that God sustains the person of faith.

Wes Eby, mission education coordinator for Nazarene Missions International, and David Hayse, World Mission Department, provided important guidance. I thank them. My wife, Judi, often served as a sounding board as I sorted through the myriad of ways to recount the story.

An evening with Ted and Mima Hughes provided rich details. Thanks to Ellen Bustle who hosted us that evening. Our time together was abbreviated by the first winter storm of the season. We could have talked much longer if we weren't concerned about slick roads.

I appreciate the insights of Dwight Rich, Joan Wilson, Charles Gates, and Ron Renshaw. Each participated as God's agents in various parts of the story. Kara Lyons in the Nazarene Archives, Karen Jones at Nazarene Missions International, and Judy Veigl and Cindy Pusey in the General Secretary's office provided documents and photos. Bob Thomas helped snatch still photos from videotapes.

Dozens of people selflessly worked to gain Don's release. Most remain unnamed in this book, a conscious decision in an attempt to keep the account uncluttered and story line moving forward. After living with this manuscript for a few months, I came to a deep appreciation for what they did during a most difficult time. Those involved in the unfolding of this drama have my utmost respect for being courageous and bold. Your dependence on the God of grace and mercy inspires me.

During one of the early meetings of the crisis management team in Quito, negotiator Chuck Howard said, "Don't forget in the darkness what God promised in the light, and don't forget in the light what God did in the darkness." In this book we remember 14 dark days in December 1995, but also rejoice that God shattered darkness with *Shouts at Sunrise.*

1

ABDUCTED

Don lay quietly. The grueling night ended on a wooden, slightly raised platform in the back of a rough, two-room cabin. Four men slept on the floor around him, another in the doorway, their bodies guarding against an escape attempt. Don closed his eyes, yet restful sleep never came.

The room lacked windows, but before long Don could see enough light through the door to realize morning had come. He asked for permission to relieve himself. Guided out the door, Don tried to get his bearings. The land around the small dwelling looked to serve as a logging operation. Logs lay in disarray with brush scattered around the clearing. An area covered by a roof on tall poles—no walls— stood off to the side, evidently a shelter under which woodcutters could work.

With a better view of the cabin, he saw that it provided only the most basic protection from the Andean climate. The rough-hewn wood siding might block the wind, but not the cold. The metal roof could shield from the rain, but not the dampness that hung in the air.

Don thanked his guard for allowing him to take care of his personal needs. He already had decided to act with courtesy at all times in an attempt to placate his abductors. Maybe he could arouse some sense of compassion within them and minimize the risk of torture. A short time later he overheard the guards mocking his polite words. Days would drag by before he heard laughter again. Don already knew that these guys were serious about their work —dead serious.

Kidnapped

December 10, 1995, started like a typical day for missionary Don Cox. For the past five years Don had worked with finances for the regional office team in Quito, Ecuador. Prior to that, he and his family served in Chile for 12 years. Don and his wife, Cheryl, still had three boys living at home with their oldest son attending Olivet Nazarene University.

Another missionary left the country before being able to sell a car—a two-door, five-passenger vehicle. As business administrator, Don was the logical choice to complete the process. He parked the car at a visible location on the campus of Seminario Teologico Nazareno (Nazarene Theological Seminary) on the north side of Quito. Very few people who saw the "for sale" sign asked for information. One caller, though, was insistent on seeing the car that day.

Don telephoned Cheryl about 4:30 that afternoon to tell her that he was going to meet someone in-

The campus of Seminario Teologico Nazareno

terested in the vehicle, attend the evening church service, then go to the airport to meet a departing missionary for whom he had some cash. Cheryl, not feeling well, decided to stay home that evening. She hung up the telephone not expecting to see Don until late that night.

About 5:15 P.M. Don met three people who came to look at the car. They appeared to have the means to make such a purchase. Their dress suggested that they came from the upper-middle class, and their speech reflected more than a rudimentary education. A man in his early 30s, a

> After a visual inspection, the spokesman suggested they take a test-drive.

little heavier than the others, served as the leader of the group. The other man and woman seemed a bit younger.

After a visual inspection, the spokesman suggested they take a test-drive. Reluctantly, Don agreed to a short one because of his other responsibilities that evening. The leader of the group took the driver's seat, and they headed southwest toward the heart of Quito before turning north toward San Antonio. Don suggested returning to the seminary campus, but the driver insisted they go on. A short ways down the road, the driver stopped to pick up two "mechanics." Don allowed them to climb past him into the backseat. As they sped away, the abductors grabbed Don and pulled him into the backseat. Don vomited.

The woman placed paper between Don's eyes and the lenses of his glasses to block his vision. One of the "mechanics" took the front passenger seat, leaving Don wedged in the backseat between two men. The kidnappers now had complete control—or so they thought.

Once they reached San Antonio, the driver turned west toward Los Bancos. After almost an hour he eased the car off the road. The mechanics, now clearly thugs, dragged Don from the car. While Don stood on the side of the road, vision still blocked by the paper blinders, the three phony car buyers started back the way they came. As the sound of the car's engine faded in the distance, the surrounding silence caused Don to hear a roar of anxiety within.

Midnight Mountain Trek

By now it had been dark for about an hour. The thugs removed the paper blinders from Don's eyes and commanded him to walk ahead of them into the Andean forest. For a half hour they trudged, each step taking Don farther from his family. They abruptly stopped. For the next five hours Don sat on the ground, huddled in a blanket provided by the men.

Several other conspirators quietly joined the trio about midnight. One family lived in the area, and the kidnappers didn't want to arouse suspicion. As they prepared to move on, three men went ahead as scouts. Whistles kept the main party informed and on track.

At first the hike was fairly easy, if a midnight trek in the Ecuadorian Andes can be so described. They followed a trail probably used by cattle to get down to a stream. Two side-by-side logs formed a foot bridge across the flowing water. If Don had been on a leisurely mountain hike with his sons, he could have traversed the log bridge with little effort. Under duress and in the dead of night, however, Don hugged the logs and pulled himself across on his belly, ripping his suit coat. Don willingly sacrificed his coat to grip the security of wood.

> Don hugged the logs and pulled himself across on his belly, ripping his suit coat.

Once across the bridge, the trek became more strenuous. No longer on a trail, the renegades started through dense underbrush. Sometimes Don found it

The cabin where Don was held the first night

hard to establish good footing in the rain-soaked soil. As they started up the side of a mountain, Don grabbed branches or vines to pull himself ahead. He climbed for several minutes and then rested. Climb. Rest. Climb. Rest. The abductors patiently waited for Don to catch his breath, then continued the ascent.

For almost four hours they moved higher, zigging and zagging, until they came to a clearing at the top of the mountain. Someone pushed Don into the cabin and onto a platform in the back room. He lay down, glad the climb was over, but anxious with the thought that he stood at the end of the road.

Forest Womb

The first morning the abductors gave Don a cup of coffee and a piece of bread for breakfast. Don thanked them. He assumed the cabin would be his cell for as long as the kidnappers held him against his will.

As daylight fully formed, two men commanded Don to start down the mountainside. Don wondered if a forced march through the dense forest would be his daily experience as a means to elude the police who hopefully were looking for him. He had gone a little more than 200 yards when he came to a platform extending from the mountainside. A log created the base against the mountain. Two trees stood on the downhill side with a small log lashed horizontally to form a goalpost support. Five cherrywood planks, one end placed on the log and the other on the goalpost, formed a floor about three feet wide and six feet long.

The guards ordered Don to sit down on the platform. "Wait here," one commanded.

A canopy of trees towered above him; dense vegetation surrounded him in all directions. The forest womb failed to comfort Don as he sat—alone.

2
DISBELIEF TO DREAD

Cheryl's blood turned ice-cold. The mixture of shock and fear exploded in disbelief.

"Could you repeat that?" she asked the telephone caller.

"We have your husband on a private property of ours. We want money. Do *not* go to the police. And do *not* tell anyone, or there will be problems. Do you understand?"

"Who are you?" Cheryl asked, her voice strangled by anxiety.

"FARC."

The caller's response tightened her chest as well as her throat. Cheryl immediately recognized the acronym of the Revolutionary Armed Forces of Colombia. The border with Colombia was not that far to the northeast. The standard operating procedure of FARC included kidnapping.

"I'll call you tomorrow night at eight." The phone went dead with a click.

Cheryl's agonizing scream brought her son Matt

rushing to her side. Matt with bronchitis had not gone to church that evening. Ron, a neighbor who was using the Cox's computer to write a Christmas letter, hurried to investigate.

"They've taken Don." The story spilled out as Cheryl frantically paced the floor. "He said they are part of FARC . . . that I should get the money . . . and not tell the police or anyone else . . . or they will hurt Don."

Help!

Ron ran to his upstairs apartment to get his wife, Judy, who rushed to comfort Cheryl. As Ron heard Cheryl weeping, he became the first of many intercessors to plead Don's case before God.

Cheryl called the South America (SAM) regional office in Quito. No answer. She then called Louie Bustle, the director of World Mission, in the United States. No answer. Stunned, she paced the floor in a daze.

Questions—countless questions —quickly dominated her disbelief. *What are we going to do? Who has him? Does Don have his glasses? He can't see without them!*

Cheryl called the regional office again. This time Liliana, the wife of Bruno Radi, the SAM regional director, answered.

The repeated sound of the acronym FARC punctured all optimism like a dart thrown at balloons.

"They've kidnapped Don!"

Liliana went right to work. She called the attorney who worked with the church who called the special police unit that dealt with kidnap cases.

Soon the apartment was full of people ready to assist. Sons Mike and Phil had returned from church. They called teachers from their school who immediately came to support the boys. The attorney and police officials started crisis management procedures. Friends entered the apartment with hugs and provided much needed strength just through their presence.

The whirlwind in Cheryl's mind kept sleep safely at a distance. Round and round the tornado tattered Cheryl's heart.

Questions consumed the conversation. The repeated sound of the acronym FARC punctured all optimism like a dart thrown at balloons.

Just that morning in the church service, the Cox family had joined the congregation in prayer for three Christian missionaries held by FARC in Colombia. Sometimes months would go by without communication from their kidnappers. The hope of the hostages' release diminished with each passing day.

Now someone who claimed to be with FARC held Don against his will. Disbelief turned to dread.

Long Night

As people began to recognize that they had

done as much as they could for the time being, they started going home for the night. Cheryl and the boys tried to get some sleep. She decided to rest in the recliner. Matt lay in a sleeping bag on the floor near his mother. Phil was on the sofa. Mike went to his bed.

The whirlwind in Cheryl's mind kept sleep safely at a distance. *Where was Don? Was he cold? What if we never see him again? Will we have to leave Ecuador? Does he have his glasses?* Round and round the tornado tattered Cheryl's heart.

Cheryl fought back with faith as she tightly gripped Psalm 121 through the long night.

I lift up my eyes to the hills—
  where does my help come from?
My help comes from the LORD,
  the Maker of heaven and earth (vv. 1-2).

As much as she appreciated the hugs of her friends, their compassion did not fill the void. The police were not all-powerful; the attorney was not all-knowing. Cheryl needed help from the Lord God Almighty.

He will not let your foot slip—
  he who watches over you will not slumber;
indeed, he who watches over Israel
  will neither slumber nor sleep.
The LORD watches over you (vv. 3-5*a*).

That promise from our faithful God cradled Cheryl as she waited for morning.

3

SIMPLE STRENGTH

As Don surveyed the forest around him, he wondered how he could survive in the quietly brutal environment. Quito sits in a valley between two mountain ranges. The valley has an elevation of more than 9,000 feet. After an hour's drive and a four-hour midnight mountain trek, Don sat in the middle of the Andean rain forest. The average temperature in this part of the world is about 57 degrees Fahrenheit year-round. Rainfall averages about 55 inches annually. The suit he had put on for church the previous morning and the blanket now wrapped around his shoulders seemed insufficient for the cool, damp climate.

A greater concern quickly took precedence—mosquitoes. The dark-skinned kidnappers didn't seem desirable to the pests, but Don's light skin shone like a beacon on a foggy December evening. An earlier encounter with mosquitoes had led to infected bites and a round of antibiotics. Don sat on the platform for only a few minutes when he began to develop a strategy to protect his skin.

Don noticed that one of the guards had an extra shirt tucked in his pants. It looked like an athletic shirt made out of nylon mesh. Perhaps Don's courtesy had aroused a semblance of compassion because, when asked, the man gave Don his shirt. Don draped the mesh shirt over his head as a mosquito net, tucking it in his jacket collar. Pulling his hands inside his suit jacket, Don sat back on the platform.

Don's cocoon did not block the sound of insects in search of prey.

Other anti-mosquito measures soon followed. Tired of holding his hands drawn up in his coat sleeves, Don hid his hands under the blanket that wrapped his body. Eventually he used vines as a rope to hold the blanket in place. His abductors later provided masking tape that Don used to cinch his pant legs closed at the ankles. They brought him a can of insect repellent, followed by a second and third.

Don's cocoon did not block the sound of insects in search of prey. Nothing quieted the incessant buzzing. The constant hum irritated the ears and tormented the mind even with all skin carefully hidden. Except for about an hour in the middle of the night and another hour in the middle of the day, Don lived with the annoying buzz of perpetual pests. Hour after hour, day after day, he sat on the platform as the mosquitoes searched for a chink in his blanket armor.

Held for Ransom

At first the kidnappers told Don they intended to hold him a couple of days. A friend, they claimed, had been mistreated. The government held the perpetrator and intended to release him without punishment. The gang abducted Don to "encourage" the government to deal justly with the offender. The pressure of his kidnapping should persuade the government to act appropriately, and then he would be released.

Don didn't buy the story.

Throughout the ordeal the kidnappers kept telling Don that he would soon be freed. If that was true, Don reasoned, then he might be able to describe the criminals to the law enforcement officers. Without making it obvious, Don started noting distinctive characteristics of each of his abductors. He memorized the type of pants and shoes worn by each person as well as other individual traits. Don gave each person a number identification.

Number 1 was the man who pretended to be interested in purchasing the car. He drove the vehicle and obviously was in charge. Don never saw him after being dropped off alongside the highway on Sunday night.

Number 2 was the other man who came to see the car. Don soon discovered that he served as the negotiator for the gang. He said his name was Omar. He came to the mountain hideout every other day or so. Number 3 was the woman who dropped the paper blinders behind Don's glasses. She may have been married to Omar, but that was just speculation on Don's part. She came to the mountain on the first Tuesday of his captivity; Don never saw her after that.

Numbers 4 and 5 were the "mechanics." Don soon learned that they were the thugs who did the dirty work, like mutilating a kidnapped victim. Number 4, the tallest and most fearsome of the two, was around during the whole ordeal, but Don never saw Number 5 after they hiked to the top of the mountain that first night.

Number 6, who stayed close to Don the first week, was obviously in charge of the guard detail. He alone kept a ski mask over his face at all times, but he was the most friendly of the kidnappers. He spoke quite proudly of the fact that no kidnapped victim had ever been harmed under his watch, something that others in the group couldn't claim. In fact, Number 6 asserted, the others would not hesitate to torture their victims. He told Don not to worry because other abducted persons had been released after as little as $30,000 had been paid in ransom. "You'll be fine," he assured Don. Don remained unconvinced. Number 6 slept under the platform the first week.

Number 7 slept under the platform too. Numbers 8 and 9 were guards stationed in the clearing

Omar finally told the expatriate missionary the truth: Don was being held for ransom.

where the cabin stood. Numbers 10 and 11 were a married couple. She did the cooking the first week. The guard detail changed at the beginning of the second week with Numbers 12, 13, 14, and 15 replacing others. The group may have had additional members; Don wasn't quite sure.

On December 11, the second day of the ordeal, Omar finally told the expatriate missionary the truth: Don was being held for ransom. The next day Omar revealed the amount they demanded for his safe release: $500,000. Don's countenance dropped.

Dead. I'm dead! Half million dollars! No one will pay that kind of money for my release. Don knew the gang would kill him—eventually—after the thrill of torturing him dissipated.

Just after Omar gave Don the disheartening news, he directed Don to speak into a small cassette tape recorder. About 11 o'clock that morning, Don read the script prepared for him as the machine recorded his emotionless voice. He had been given permission the afternoon before to write a letter to Cheryl. On Tuesday they confiscated the letter because he wrote it in English. Since they did not read English, they could not censor what Don wrote. He rewrote the letter in Spanish.

Power in Prayer, Strength in the Scriptures

After Omar left with the tape recording, Don asked Number 6 for permission to pray aloud. The psalmist David wrote:

"Hear my cry, O God;
   listen to my prayer.
From the ends of the earth I call to you,
   I call as my heart grows faint;
   lead me to the rock that is higher than I"
                                (Psalm 61:1-2).

Don needed to combat a fainting heart, so he asked to be allowed to cry out to the Lord. Permission granted, soon Don's prayers filled the forest canopy as if it were a camp-meeting tent.

Emboldened by the privilege to pray aloud, the next day Don requested and received permission to read the Bible. Don always carried a New Testament with Psalms and Proverbs that he received from a member of the Gideons several years before in Chile. Being confined to the platform in the rain forest, Don rejoiced that he habitually slipped God's Word in his pocket each morning.

The Proverbs only irritated Don. He longed for deliverance, not wisdom.

Don started with the Gospel of John. "In the beginning was the Word, and the Word was with God, and the Word was God" (John 1:1). Verse by verse Don found strength for his soul even as his body faced duress. Since his guards listened as Don read, he judiciously skipped verses like John 10:9-10a, "I am the gate; whoever enters through me will be saved. He will come in and go out, and find pasture. The thief comes only to steal and kill and destroy." That last verse seemed a little too per-

The New Testament Don read while kidnapped

sonal for public airing in the present circumstance.

The Proverbs only irritated Don, so he skipped that section in his reading. He longed for deliverance, not wisdom.

When Don finished reading John, he continued through the Book of Acts. He then doubled back to read the synoptic gospels. He turned to the back of the New Testament to read about love in the three letters written by John before rejoicing for the ultimate victory promised in Revelation.

The men who guarded Don heard everything he read. As Don read the letters written by Paul, his situation mirrored that of the apostle as he wrote to the Philippians: "As a result, it has become clear throughout the whole palace guard and to everyone else that I am in chains for Christ" (1:13). Just as the Roman soldiers heard the gospel declared while keeping an eye on Paul, so the kidnappers near Don heard the Good News. The platform in the rain forest became a pulpit.

Since Ecuador sits on the equator (the Spanish word for equator is *ecuador*), sunrise occurs a few minutes before or after six o'clock year-round. Likewise, changing seasons adjust sunset only a few minutes. This rhythm pervades all year—12 hours of daylight, 12 hours of darkness.

Don established a rhythm of his own as he lay on the mountainside. About six o'clock each evening as he settled into the sleeping bag and positioned the blankets appropriately, Don prayed. The simple prayer he learned as a child seemed the most appropriate given the circumstances:

> Now I lay me down to sleep.
> I pray Thee, Lord, my soul to keep.
> If I should die . . .

4
ABANDONMENT

Time seemed to stand still while Cheryl and others waited for the next telephone call from the kidnappers. Sure, many details screamed for attention, many people clamored for information, many decisions begged to be made. The cacophony, however, did little to propel the process forward. Only a conversation with Omar could do that, but his calls were too brief and too infrequent to get a sense of progress. The effort to gain Don's release felt like a stalemate from the beginning.

Finding someone to take Omar's calls became the primary order of business for Monday, December 11th. The head of the special police unit instructed Cheryl not to talk with the abductors, something she gladly accepted. But who would do it? They had just a few hours to get a negotiator in place before the call scheduled for 8:00 P.M. Personnel at the Church of the Nazarene International Headquarters in Kansas City would assist with this task.

One of the first contacts made by the World Mission Department was with Crisis Consulting International (CCI), an organization whose consultants serve as advisors and hostage negotiators for Christian organizations. The executive director of CCI knew of a man trained in critical incident negotiations who worked with another mission agency in Quito. Carlos agreed to serve, but he was available only four days.

Cheryl knew Carlos. Their children attended the same school and participated together on sports teams. Both Cheryl and Carlos sang in the choir made up of missionaries and others from the community. They performed once a year, the first weekend of December, as part of the founding of Quito celebration. Cheryl had confidence in Carlos.

As the clock marched past eight and toward nine, everyone grew more anxious.

Several friends gathered as the 8:00 hour approached that Monday evening. Speculation punctuated the conversation, but no one had much confidence in what they imagined. As the clock marched past eight and toward nine, everyone grew more anxious. Why didn't the call come through as scheduled? Had the kidnappers discovered that the police were involved? Was Don still alive?

At 9:10 the phone rang. The room became deathly still. Carlos took a deep breath and picked up the receiver.

The apartment building where the Coxes lived in 1995

"My name is Carlos. With whom am I speaking?"

"Eh . . . with Omar."

"Amal?"

"O . . . Omar. I think that you are the one responsible to talk with me. Is that right?"

"Yes, I am a friend of the family."

"OK."

"As you can understand, the woman is very distraught."

"Yes."

"She asked me, as a friend of the family, to speak with you. OK?"

"No problem."

"It's extremely important that I have some test that I am talking with the proper person."

"Look, Carlos, look . . ."

"In second place, it's necessary to know that our friend Don is in good health."

"Yes, I can guarantee that."

"Good. This is essential to know."

Everyone in the room gained a degree of confidence as they heard the firm tone of Carlos's words. He controlled the conversation so far. Carlos continued.

"We need some kind of test so that we can continue talking."

"What do you need that I can bring you?"

"For example, if possible, I would like to talk with him."

"It's impossible."

"There's no way?"

"It's not possible because he . . . the cellular won't reach there . . . practically he is in another country."

"Well, I understand that this can be a problem, but tell me this, if you can converse with him and pass messages . . ."

"Look, to converse it takes me a day to go and another to return."

". . . because if you could, for example, ask him where he spent his honeymoon, something of this nature."

"I will ask him."

With that request, the first proof-of-life test began.

The conversation continued as Omar instructed Carlos to have a cellular telephone ready to use the next morning at nine o'clock. Carlos insisted that he could not meet that demand since all stores were closed for the night, so Omar agreed to call the apartment again. Omar reiterated his demand that they not bring the police into the negotiations. Carlos stated that he understood Omar's requirement but did not comment one way or the other. Omar didn't need to know about the many people already at work to liberate Don and capture the perpetrators.

Crisis Management Teams

The church formed two crisis management teams, one in Quito and the other in Kansas City. The team in Quito was led by a representative of the church who arrived within 24 hours of the initial Sunday evening call. Other missionaries assisted with logistical matters, including setting up equipment to record the telephone conversations. In addition to the security officer from the U.S. Embassy in Quito, the United States government provided three critical incident experts to serve as advisors, the first of whom arrived less than 24 hours after the kidnapping. Two representatives from CCI traveled to Quito to counsel the church during the negotiations. Since the kidnapping occurred within their jurisdiction, the special police unit from Ecuador led the law enforcement effort.

Another person led the crisis management team in Kansas City. Channels for communication with the church constituents and press were established.

Members of the World Mission Literature staff transcribed and translated recorded telephone conversations. A retired missionary accepted an assignment to care for the extended Cox family, calling them daily with updates and offering encouragement. The Board of General Superintendents received daily briefings and held conference calls to make strategic decisions. The team in Kansas City began planning for the long term, not knowing how long the ordeal might last.

The morning after the abduction someone called the regional office with a brief message: "The car we took last night is on a street in Calderon." Calderon is a city on the road to Colombia that was in the opposite direction from the mountain hideout. They tried to support their prior claim that Don had been moved to Colombia under the control of FARC. Police officers and church representatives retrieved the car, but it did not yield any clues.

Omar called at nine o'clock on Tuesday morning just as he promised. Since he did not yet have answers for the proof-of-life test, the conversation did not last long. Once again Omar insisted that Carlos get a cellular phone to use in the negotiations. Omar agreed to call again on Wednesday afternoon.

Carlos arrived at the house around noon on Wednesday. For several hours he just sat and waited. Finally about 8:00 P.M. the phone rang. Carlos answered it.

"Good evening. The home of the Coxes."

"Good evening. With whom am I speaking?"

"With Carlos."

"Eh, Carlos, how are you? This is Omar."

"With whom am I speaking?"

"Omar greets you."

"How are you, Omar? I was waiting all afternoon as we had talked about."

"OK. Look then, they were married in Peoria, Illinois, 19 of February 1969."

Omar seemed to begin reading from notes as he continued. "We spent the honeymoon night in Bloomington, Illinois. Afterward we returned to our home in Indiana. Is that OK?"

Carlos covered the telephone receiver and looked to Cheryl for confirmation that the information was correct. Their wedding was in January, but the other information was accurate.

Cheryl's heart sank. This latest threat only bolstered her fears.

Cheryl whispered "yes," then excitedly turned to the boys to tell them of the proof that their father remained alive. Her joy evaporated, however, as the conversation continued.

"What we need is a half million dollars."

"I understand what you are saying."

"OK."

"I will have to inform the people here because I can only tell the family what you tell me. They will have to make whatever decision. OK?"

"Tomorrow I will call you for the answer because the year is about to end, and I am in a little bit of a hurry, brother. If not then, I am going to call you next year."

Cheryl's heart sank. From the beginning of this ordeal she feared that the telephone calls would stop. This latest threat only bolstered her fears. And the amount of the ransom: $500,000. How could they meet such a demand? They personally didn't have that amount of money. The church had a no-ransom policy, so funds would not come from that source. When Omar called the next day, she knew Carlos could not say what Omar wanted to hear. Don's murder couldn't be far behind.

What a cruel assault to Cheryl's emotions! One moment she swung on a sliver of hope, the next she fell into the pit filled with utter despair. Carlos hung up the telephone. The tortuous wait for Omar's next call began.

The downward spiral dragged Cheryl lower the next day. Between 10 and 11 in the morning, flowers were delivered to the seminary office. Tucked in the flowers was a tape recording Don made two days before, a note from Omar, and a letter Don wrote to Cheryl. Church representatives took the package with them to the U.S. Embassy. In a three-hour meeting they reviewed all the information they had gathered and explored options to be considered. The critical incident experts expressed their grave concern with the rapid pace the kidnappers set. They needed to slow the process to a more regulated stride if at all possible, or else Don would probably be lost in the frantic plunge.

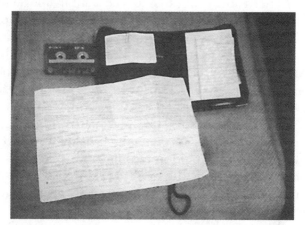

The contents of the first package *(clockwise from top left)*: cassette tape, Omar's note, and Don's letter to Cheryl

When the church officials left the U.S. Embassy, they went to see Cheryl. She listened to the tape recording. Later that day, after coming home from school, Phil insisted that he be allowed to hear it. Cheryl took him into a bedroom and played the tape. They looked at each other as they heard Don's voice. Slow. Deliberate. Monotone. Lifeless.

"Mom, what are we going to do?" Phil pleaded. Cheryl didn't have an answer for her youngest son.

Huddled in the Dark

Carlos waited for the telephone call from Omar on Thursday evening. When it came, for an inexplicable reason, a female police officer forcibly took the telephone. Anyone with knowledge of the intricacies of hostage negotiation knows that it is best to utilize only one negotiator. This time, however, Carlos helplessly listened as another talked with Omar.

"Hello."

"Hi. Is Carlos there?"

"Eh, yes. Who is calling?"

"Omar."

"Just a moment please. (muttered) Eh, Carlos? (To Omar) Ah, just a moment. Please wait for him because he is in the bathroom."

"Mmm."

"Or you can call him in a couple of minutes."

"Good. I'll call back later."

"Eh, OK."

"Just a question. To whom do I speak?"

"With the maid."

"What is your name?"

"Raquel."

As the conversation continued, the radios of other police officers in the room crackled to life. Telephone workers had traced the call. The police hustled out of the apartment and raced down the street. Cheryl groaned inwardly because Omar likely heard the commotion caused by radios and slammed doors.

Cheryl stuffed her rage until the call was over and then exploded.

Cheryl stuffed her rage until the call was over and then exploded. "You just got my husband killed," she screamed at the police officer.

"You just got my husband killed," she screamed at the police officer. "We don't have a maid. Don doesn't know anybody by the name of Raquel. They're going to ask him about Raquel, and when he can't answer their questions, they'll kill him."

Cheryl sobbed uncontrollably. Never had she felt so hopeless—so helpless.

The police arrived at the telephone Omar used that night moments too late. They just missed the apprehension of the kidnapper that everyone so desperately desired.

Friends stayed with Cheryl and the boys until everyone's emotions subsided a bit. Then they left for the night.

Cheryl settled into the recliner to try to get some sleep. The only sleep she had had all week was the six hours she pieced together two nights before. Even through the utter exhaustion, her mind and body kept churning.

The phone rang about 11:50 P.M. Cheryl answered it. When she recognized Omar's voice, she immediately started shaking—violent shaking. *I'm not supposed to talk to this guy,* she thought.

"Is Carlos there?"

"No, he had to leave."

"When will he be back?"

"I don't know."

"Who are you?"

Cheryl hesitated. She couldn't tell him her real identity. She didn't know what Omar might do if he thought she was home alone.

"I'm the maid."

"What's your name?"

"Raquel."

Omar seemed satisfied with the answer.

As soon as Cheryl hung up, she grabbed a cellular phone. In the darkened apartment, she crawled under the dining room table and dialed the special police unit. The officer assured her that she was safe, implying that her apartment was under surveillance by law enforcement officers.

Cheryl called the Radi's house. "I can't stay here," she cried. "Please come and get me and the boys."

Sleep never came that night, but Cheryl felt less afraid away from her own home.

Cheryl thoughtfully prepared a "release kit" for Don. With each item she packed, however, hope seemed more deeply buried.

Sad Day

The boys finished their final exams on Friday, just before the Christmas vacation began. They had made the decision earlier in the week that the family would leave Ecuador on Saturday. Cheryl spent Friday packing, including things that reminded her of Don. She packed the clock given to them by their home church on their 25th wedding anniversary. She decided she didn't have room in the suitcases to take the family photos, so she boxed and gave them to a friend for safekeeping. Warm clothes necessary for Peoria in December took precedence.

Cheryl thoughtfully prepared a "release kit" for Don. He would need clothes and personal items should he be freed. With each item she packed, however, hope seemed more deeply buried.

After a spaghetti dinner with friends and teachers and an evening for saying good-bye, Cheryl once again settled into the recliner to rest. Matt curled up on the floor nearby, Phil slept on the couch, and Mike went to his bed. Overcome with grief, Cheryl woke the boys sobbing.

"Are you OK, Mom?"

No, she was *not* OK. The pain overwhelmed her.

As they drove to the airport on Saturday morning, Cheryl wondered if they would ever return to Quito. The boys were leaving home to go to the United States. Would they be able to come back to Ecuador?

As they stood in line just before boarding the airplane, a woman stepped up and placed her hand on Cheryl's shoulder. "I know who you are," she whispered. "I've prayed for you all week." With that the woman slipped back to her place in the line.

Cheryl looked around wondering if anyone else recognized her and the boys. She most feared someone with intent on snagging them like they had Don.

Concern for her own safety came with feelings that she was abandoning Don. She felt like she had given up and walked away in his hour of greatest need. Cheryl knew in her head that leaving Ecuador was the wise thing to do, but her heart wasn't convinced yet.

44

The Cox family—well, most of it—flew from Quito to Miami then on to Chicago and Peoria. During the flight Cheryl began to relax for the first time in a week. She started feeling safe. She stopped scanning every face suspiciously.

Cheryl went to sleep in Peoria at 11 o'clock Saturday night. She awoke the next morning 12 hours after going to bed. Finally rest had come to her weary body.

5
DREARY DAYS

On Friday afternoon, the sixth day of Don's captivity, the cook and her husband known to Don as Numbers 10 and 11 replaced Numbers 6 and 7 as guards at the platform for a couple of hours. Earlier in the week Number 10 shot a bird that Number 11 used to make a soup for Don. Among other areas of interest she wanted to know if Don preferred more salt on his food.

Her concern arose from selfish motivation. Don's health and well-being would impact her own. If Don became sick because of the food, she would likely be punished, maybe even tortured and killed. If he remained reasonably healthy, she could quietly complete her task.

From the beginning of the ordeal Don suffered physically. The coffee they gave him irritated his stomach. He requested hot tea instead, which was provided. Most days he carried a queasy feeling in his gut.

Anxiety settled in his bowels. Diarrhea became

a constant companion. The abductors cleared a section about 20 feet from the platform for use as a toilet area. Realizing that open sewage could create serious consequences, on each trip Don tore a large leaf from a colocasia plant, commonly known as elephant ear, to use as a toilet bowl. The abductors provided tissue paper. Don folded the leaf to create an envelope around the excrement, then tossed it as far down the mountainside as he could.

Given his perpetual diarrhea, Don realized that dehydration posed a real threat. He drank water regularly, yet rationed his consumption so he would not exhaust the supply. Don feared that additional water might not be provided.

Breakfast often consisted of bread with jam or fruit, such as banana, orange, or grapes. Other meals might include rice, potatoes, or soup. Once they offered him pudding in a plastic cup, but it nauseated Don, so he gave it to the guard. Another time they brought rotisserie-roasted chicken from Ecuador's version of KFC. Often Don forced himself to eat a little bit, even though he didn't feel like doing so, to ward off at least a few of the health risks he faced.

With the negotiating process already charged with suspicion, this deception did not help.

False Promises

As they talked that Friday afternoon, Numbers 10 and 11 told Don that they were walking out on

Sunday. They excitedly said that they believed he would walk out with them. Just the day before Number 6 told Don that someone had deposited money in an account for his release. Don did not believe that to be true. He knew neither his family nor the church would do such a thing. Yet, maybe the negotiations had progressed.

Omar showed up on Saturday morning, Day 7. He asked Don to identify Carlos, the man representing Don's family in the negotiations. Don said that Carlos was a family friend. Then Omar asked about Raquel. Don didn't know a Raquel. Omar asked about the family's maid. Don said the family didn't have a maid. Don could not confirm what Omar had been told two nights before. With the negotiating process already charged with suspicion, this deception did not help. But would it hurt Don's chance for a safe release?

After Omar's visit, Don contemplated what he might do to help the police find this place should he be released. Just then a passenger plane flew overhead. Don was in the flight path of planes leaving the airport in Quito, probably planes that took off to the north, then looped to the west before flying south to Guayaquil. Don noted the time on the watch still strapped to his wrist. Maybe aviation authorities could review the course of airplanes to narrow the search for the kidnapper's camp. A second plane and a second time were noted. Then a third. Before he went to sleep that night, Don had stored in his memory five times when planes flew overhead.

The business card on which Don encoded the times that planes flew overhead

When he awoke the next morning, Don grew a little concerned that he might forget the flight times. Writing down the hours and minutes might arouse suspicion, so Don devised a code. He took a business card on which he had already written four Scripture references. He would add five more. The flight overhead at 1:20 P.M. became Revelation 1:20 on his card, followed by Revelation 3:21 and John 3:31 for flights at 3:21 and 3:31 respectively. The airplane overhead at 5:51 posed a bit of a problem because Don could not find a fifth chapter with a 51st verse. His entry became Lucas (Luke) 5:25, 26. When Don heard the fifth flight of the afternoon, a guard stood nearby, so he didn't risk looking at his watch. He later estimated the time to be somewhere between 10 and 15 minutes after six o'clock. Don jotted John 6:10-15 on his card.

Packing to Stay Put

As predicted by Numbers 10 and 11, the order came to break camp on Sunday morning. They removed the plastic tarp stretched above the platform to keep Don dry. Don rolled the sleeping bag and foam mat on which he slept. Numbers 6 and 7 gathered up some of the items and hiked up the hill to the clearing, leaving Don sitting under a tree.

Don sat there all day. Nothing came of his anticipation. The people who guarded him the first week walked down the mountain after reinforcements arrived. They left Don behind.

> **Don sat in solitary confinement. One moment lumbered forward to the next. Boredom bloomed.**

Don looked at the new guards with suspicion. Number 6 warned that others had a tendency toward torture. Would the terror and pain he experienced escalate dramatically?

As nightfall approached and it appeared he was staying put, Don asked if they were going to reinstall the plastic tarp above his platform. They did. Later that week a heavy rainstorm blew over the mountain. The tarp kept Don dry, which probably would not have happened the way it had been installed the week before.

Don huddled under the tarp as the fury of the storm pounded the mountain hideout. To keep the

50

water from washing across the platform, someone had dug a drain hole on the outside of the log base against the mountain. Water rushing down the mountainside from the daily rains hit the log, then escaped through the drain hole as it made its way farther down the mountain. Don kept the drain clear of mud and debris.

Don missed the companionship of Number 6 as a new week began. Number 12 replaced him as the leader of the guards. Number 13 joined Number 12 to sleep under the platform at night, but soon after daybreak they both climbed up to the clearing. The platform could be seen from there, so they performed their duty from that vantage point. Number 14 or Number 15 would bring meals to Don but never lingered to talk.

Don sat in solitary confinement. One moment lumbered forward to the next. Mosquitoes threatened their intentions with incessant buzzing. Boredom bloomed.

On most mornings, someone brought breakfast to Don about eight o'clock. On Tuesday, December 19th, no one appeared with food at the usual time. Don listened. Nothing. He heard no activity in the clearing. Could it be that the gang had abandoned him? Don tuned his ear for evidence until he called out around 10:00. Hope for liberation crumbled when one of the guards answered. The person bringing the food up the mountain had not arrived yet.

Disappointed, Don settled in for another dreary day.

6
DEEPENING SHADOWS

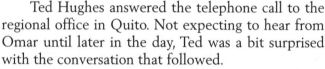

Ted Hughes answered the telephone call to the regional office in Quito. Not expecting to hear from Omar until later in the day, Ted was a bit surprised with the conversation that followed.

"Good morning. Is Cheryl there?"

"Who?"

"The wife of Don Cox."

"No, she's not here at the moment."

Ted did not tell Omar that Cheryl and the boys were on their way to Miami.

"How about Carlos?"

"No, he's not here either."

Carlos had left Ecuador too. His son was to be married in Hawaii, and Carlos departed the day before.

"Who are you?" Omar demanded.

Ted had already decided not to hide behind an alias. If the kidnappers told Don with whom they were talking, Ted hoped it would encourage Don to know that he had come to Ecuador to assist. He wanted the news of his involvement to indicate to Don that the church was working diligently to gain his release.

"My name is Ted Hughes," he told Omar. "I have been designated by the church to take over the negotiating process from Carlos." That brief interchange formed a relationship extremely critical to the process to free Don from his abductors.

Ted Hughes and his wife, Mima, retired from missionary service but continued to serve the church in various capacities. After going to Africa to meet with the regional directors, they stopped in Venezuela on their way back to the United States. Bruno Radi, regional director for South America, called Ted in Venezuela, begging him to come to Quito immediately. Fearing that the telephone lines may not be secure, Bruno did not tell Ted the nature of the crisis, only that they desperately needed his assistance.

Being the Christmas season, all flights from Venezuela to Ecuador were overbooked. So Ted and Mima returned to Miami as scheduled. As soon as they arrived in the United States, Ted called the church headquarters in Kansas City to find out the reason for the urgency and secrecy. With little hesitation, Ted accepted the call to become the negotiator for Don's release, beginning the most difficult assignment of his life.

While Mima washed clothes, Ted began his orientation. The office in Kansas City faxed documents to Ted to bring him up-to-speed. The crisis consultant gave Ted a crash course in hostage negotiation. One hour did not seem like enough time for such a critical task. Just a few hours after arriving in Miami from Venezuela, Ted boarded another plane headed for Quito, sure of the destination but not the outcome.

In Search of a Strategy

No option rose to the top as the clear choice for the negotiating strategy. Every alternative considered by the crisis management team included at least one undesirable aspect. Plus each had high risk. If they skimmed off everything undesirable or risky, they would empty the pot. Nothing simple lay ahead.

The outlaws wanted money. That's it. No political agenda. Just money.

They had learned a lot about the kidnappers as the drama unfolded. Early in the process Omar claimed they were members of FARC, a revolutionary group in neighboring Colombia. Now the authorities believed they were a local criminal gang. At first Omar intimated they held Don in Colombia. The police now suspected that Don, like the other 48 hostages in 1995, was hidden in an uninhabited area not far from Quito. As the profile of the criminals began to emerge, local authorities recognized similarities between the events of the week and previous abductions. They recognized the name Omar and the voice of the caller.

The outlaws wanted money. That's it. No political agenda. Just money. This particular group always got something too. Maybe not the original demand, but something. Families typically paid a ransom 10 to 15 days after the kidnapping.

These gangsters had a reputation for violent behavior. In prior cases, if negotiations failed to progress to the hoodlums' satisfaction, they sent an ear or finger or hand to show the family the seriousness of their demands. These guys were more than willing to mutilate and murder. Ecuadorian authorities knew that even if a family paid the ransom, the gang still might harm the victim. That had happened before. If nothing was paid, the victim would suffer for sure. They wanted money, and every imaginable grotesque act could punctuate the demand.

The goals of the crisis management team diametrically opposed the goals of these criminals. The team wanted Don's safe return; the kidnappers wouldn't shrink from tortured confinement. The church would not abandon the no-ransom policy; the gang only wanted money.

Within hours of arriving in Quito, Ted began to feel the gravity of the situation. He could not provide the only thing that would pacify the kidnappers—money. What *could* he say? Ted worried that one misstep on his part would result in the death of his good friend and missionary colleague. Never before had Ted faced a situation where the consequences of his words and actions were so grave. He longed for the insight and courage that only God could provide.

Negotiating on a Tightrope

Ted learned quickly that hostage negotiation requires discernment of nuances in the conversation. At times he had to firmly communicate that what Omar demanded would not be met, yet he couldn't slam the door shut. He always tried to keep a window of opportunity open. An abrupt "no" could prove fatal for Don.

> A man on a motorcycle pulled alongside the passenger door of the car and bent over to stare at Cheryl, his face just outside the window from hers.

Omar often spoke in code because he used public telephones to place the calls. If people overheard snatches of the conversation, they would think he was trying to close a sale. One time he pretended to negotiate the sale of an automobile. Another time he asked about the delivery of Bibles. Most often he referred to the "business" or the "product." He called the police *primos*, the Spanish word for *cousins*. Even though Omar used code words, Ted knew exactly what he meant.

In contrast, Ted and the crisis management team wondered how much Omar and the kidnappers really knew about the Cox family, the church, and the crisis management team. Omar claimed to have driven past the apartment where Don and Cheryl lived. Some suspicious people were seen in the neighborhood, but were they part of the gang or just regular folks looking for a friend's new apartment?

Other odd events caused people to wonder if they were under surveillance. Cheryl lost the filling from a tooth on December 14. A friend drove her to the dentist. While stopped in the right lane at a traffic light, a man on a motorcycle pulled alongside the passenger door of the car and bent over to stare at Cheryl, his face just outside the window from hers. The driver of the car turned right, only to have the motorcyclist follow and repeat his behavior at the next stoplight. Who was this man, and why did he stare at Cheryl?

Someone saw a photographer taking pictures of the seminary campus. A thug casing the joint? On Sunday evening, December 17, an unknown couple stopped by the Carcelén church. Their conversation with the pastor sounded a little fishy. Who were they? A man with a walkie-talkie stood across the street from another church building for several hours one day. What business did he have that required radio communication?

When church officials retrieved the car used by the kidnappers to abduct Don, they found one set of keys. They knew that Don always carried two sets of keys, including a master key that would give him access to every mission building. Who had the second set of keys?

Omar claimed to know about bank accounts. Did he have an informant in the bank? Had the abductors tortured details out of Don? Or was this just a bluff?

Violent Threats

Don's physical condition continued to cause concern for both Omar and Ted. Ted volunteered to provide medicine, but Omar rebuffed the offer. Don suffered because of anxiety and the climate, Omar claimed, so the medicine for the physical symptoms would have minimal benefit, he reasoned.

At the end of the conversation on Thursday morning, December 21, Ted asked Omar to provide a second proof of life. "I would like to know the name of Don's dog," Ted requested. Omar agreed to provide the information.

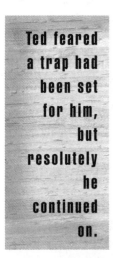

Ted feared a trap had been set for him, but resolutely he continued on.

About 24 hours later Omar had the answer. His ready response contradicted his claim that it took him a day to travel to where the men held Don and another day to return to Quito. "I want to know about the dogs of Mr. Cox, Scooter and Princess. How are they?" Omar asked. Ted confirmed that the information was correct.

They knew Don was still alive. Conversations would continue.

Then Omar told Ted that Don had a message for him. Ted—and only Ted—could pick it up at a hotel for which Omar provided directions. This development brought grave concern to the crisis management team. Omar sent the first package with a flower arrangement delivered to the seminary. Why did he require Ted to pick up the second one? Everyone realized that the risk for Ted increased exponentially with Omar's instructions. They didn't seem to have any option but to comply.

Ted and another missionary took a taxi to pick up the package. When they arrived at their destination, the other missionary stayed with the taxi while Ted went inside what appeared to be a flophouse.

Ted walked through a side entrance. Shadows dominated the long narrow passageway. Ted feared a trap had been set for him, but resolutely he continued on. A small room at the top of the stairs served as the hotel lobby. One lightbulb dangled from an electrical wire. Two tough-looking men waited for Ted behind a small table.

"I have come for a package," Ted stated. The men asked Ted to identify himself. "Hughes," he told them, "I'm Ted Hughes." They demanded to see identification. Ted showed them his passport. This created a major problem.

The name Hughes is pronounced as one syllable in English—*HYOOZ*. To see the name written, however, causes the Spanish speaker to hear a different pronunciation. Since the consonant "h" is silent in Spanish, those two letters would be ignored. A two-syllable word remains—*OO-JEHS*. Ted identified himself as Mr. *HYOOZ*. But to the two men, Ted's passport identified him as Mr. *OO-JEHS*.

After careful interrogation, Ted finally satisfied the men that he was the one to whom they were to give the package. They handed Ted a manila envelope in a black plastic bag. Ted carefully held the bag by the corner, hoping there might be fingerprints on the bag that would help the investigators. Once safely back in the taxi, Ted directed the driver on a circuitous route in case they were followed.

Once at a safe location, they carefully opened the package to find a letter from Don to Cheryl, a letter from the kidnappers to Ted, and a tape recording of Don's voice. In the letter Don acknowledged that he suffered physically. On the tape he stated that he had been feeling pressure in his chest. Those who listened wondered if anxiety might crush Don before the outlaw group would. Don begged Ted to cooperate with the kidnappers and reiterated the demand that the police not intervene. "My life is in your hands," he said to Ted, certainly a sobering message for his friend to hear.

A heaviness came over those present as they read the letter from the kidnappers. "We have been trying to negotiate diligently and humanely with you," the letter stated, "but let us warn you that our patience is coming to an end." The letter continued with the threat to harm others. The kidnappers had pushed the needle on the danger meter to the extreme. The crisis management team now had many people for whom to be concerned.

The fact that the abductors reduced the ransom demand from $500,000 to $200,000 did not encourage Ted. A 60 percent reduction might excite a Christmas shopper but not a hostage negotiator dealing with a no-ransom policy.

The letter continued: "From now on we will speak only two minutes maximum by the cellular phone. Please wait for a call on December 23, 1995, in the afternoon."

Omar called at 4:40 P.M. on that Saturday. The call lasted seven minutes.

7

RESCUED

Sabbath. God ordained the day of rest.

The events of the week leeched energy from Ted and others on the crisis management team. For hours they debated potential negotiation strategies to the point of mental fatigue. The anxiety of dealing with life-and-death issues lay heavy on their emotions. Members of the team willingly abandoned sleep, grabbing only a few hours here and there for days at a time. Their bodies ached for rest. Often the spiritual burden drove Ted to his knees beside his bed in the middle of the night.

Sunday, December 24, 1995, promised to be an oasis for the battle-weary fighters. Ted welcomed the prospect of a divinely-appointed day to rest and recharge.

Since they did not expect a telephone call from Omar, members of the crisis management team felt free to wander awhile. The gorgeous weather beckoned them to bask in the warm glow of God's creation. A walk in a nearby park loosened muscles and liberated joints held at high-alert all week. The fresh Andean air cleansed not only the body, but its fingers began to rejuvenate the soul.

The brief walk confirmed the genius of God's design. Sabbath had come. Ted and another missionary returned to their room intent on an afternoon nap.

Change of Plans

The cellular phone used for the negotiations rang a little after two o'clock. Who could be calling? Only Omar and the police had the number. Ted asked his colleague to answer the call. "If it's Omar, tell him to call again at the scheduled time," Ted instructed.

A police lieutenant. *"Rescued!* Don has been rescued," the officer said. "Meet us at the police academy on the north edge of town. Three kidnappers were killed in the operation."

Plans for a leisurely Sunday gladly tossed aside, Ted and the fellow missionary quickly prepared to head for the police academy. Renewal would come in another way this day.

Before they could rush out the door, another phone in the room rang. The crisis consultant who coached Ted through the negotiations checked in. Ted told him the good news and asked him to relay the message to church leaders in Kansas City.

Ted called their key contact at the U.S. Embassy. The official already knew and planned to meet them at the police academy.

Ted scribbled a note for members of the crisis

management team who were still out for a walk, taped it to the television in the room, and grabbed a cell phone as they headed out the door. As the men traveled, they sang along with a tape recording of "A Mighty Fortress Is Our God." With full voice they declared,

> Did we in our own strength confide,
> Our striving would be losing;
> Were not the right Man on our side,
> The Man of God's own choosing.
> Dost ask who that may be?
> Christ Jesus—it is He;
> Lord Sabaoth, His name;
> From age to age the same;
> And He must win the battle.

A continent away Cheryl and their four sons attended a worship service in her home church on Sunday morning, followed by lunch with a few family members. About 2:30 P.M. Louie Bustle called Cheryl.

"Are you sitting down? Don has been rescued!"

Cheryl shouted with delight, a very different tone than the scream she emitted on the Sunday evening two weeks before. Cheryl hugged her sister. Jumping up and down in the kitchen, the two siblings looked like two little girls at a birthday party.

Jumping up and down in the kitchen, the two siblings looked like two little girls at a birthday party.

Ted arrived at the police academy about 45 minutes after receiving the call. The events of the past 22 hours began to unfold. The night before, Ted kept Omar on the phone for seven minutes. The police traced the call like they had others, but this time they got to the location in time to identify Omar. Rather than arresting him immediately, they followed him until the opportune moment. Omar revealed where they could find Don in the mountain hideout.

Ted's cell phone rang as they stood in the parking lot at the police academy. This time it was the crisis manager in Kansas City. Should they wait to publicize the report until Ted could confirm Don's safe release?

"No," Ted replied, "the source is reliable. Share the good news!"

Once the law enforcement officers knew Don's location, they called the special police unit to duty. Negotiations seemed to be on hold because of the weekend and the Christmas holiday, so a few of the personnel from the elite unit were allowed to leave town. Some of the investigators working on the case stepped in to form a 20-member squad. They began the ascent about three in the morning. They were on-site nearly two hours later, silently assessing the situation and finalizing their plans.

Other officials arrived at the police academy while Ted listened to the story. Soon those assembled were back in their cars headed toward the mountain hideout. After crossing a mountain summit, they drove down a dangerously steep, winding road. Traveling this road took them into another world. The weather changed to cold and misty. Geological formations prevented cellular phone signals from reaching the nearest tower. So close to Quito, yet so isolated.

When the group arrived at the trailhead, Don still remained on the mountain. The police wanted to take Ted to where Don had been held, but he was dressed for church, not an hour-long hike in the rain forest. Instead, a police officer handed Ted a walkie-talkie.

"Merry Christmas, Don."

When Don replied, a cascade of gratitude poured from deep within Ted's soul. The two friends praised God together. Don assured Ted that he did not need medical attention. He was OK. They talked for 15 minutes, cut short only by an exhausted battery in the police radio.

After talking to Don on the radio, Ted drove out of the valley until he could get a signal on the cell phone. He called other members of the crisis management team, telling them the details he had learned. Ted provided directions. They hurried to cars to join the celebration on the mountainside.

Dr. Bustle called Cheryl a second time. Then a third. Each call provided more information to the ecstatic family in Peoria.

Ted learned that the special police unit launched a three-pronged attack just before daybreak. With loud shouts the forces sprang into action. Two groups subdued the kidnappers in the mountain clearing.

Down below, an officer pounced on the guard

sleeping under Don's platform. The agent squeezed the kidnapper's hand. The pistol fell away. Immobilized in an instant, no shot would be fired at Don.

Simultaneously another special forces agent rushed to Don. "Mr. Cox. We are the police. You are saved."

Rescued! I've been rescued! I'm not going to die on that mountain. I'm going to live!

A new day dawned for Don, one he scarcely dared imagine just hours before. Don began to weep —tears washed wave after wave of pent-up anxiety.

The police spent all morning conducting a detailed investigation. They called a television crew to record their success. Maybe potential kidnappers could be deterred when they saw the effectiveness of the special police unit.

Sweat dripped from Don's forehead, his hair matted, two weeks' worth of whiskers covering his face.

Dusk settled early in the deep valley as the high mountains blocked the sun. The police began walking Don out to the trailhead. At first Ted could only see flashlight beams bobbing through the trees. As the group approached those waiting, Ted caught a glimpse of his friend. Sweat dripped from Don's forehead, his hair matted, two weeks' worth of whiskers covering his face. The mesh shirt Don used to protect himself from mosquitoes curled around his neck. The blanket wrapped around

Don Cox soon after his rescue. Note the mesh shirt
on his head—the mosquito protector.

Don and Ted walking out of the rain forest

his shoulders failed to totally cover the ripped suit Don still wore. Clutching a walking stick, he looked like Moses trudging out of the wilderness.

Ted hurried to his friend. They held each other, an embrace that symbolized the strength of the bonds forged in the days just past. They wept tears of joy, artesian water rising from a depth of gratitude they had never experienced before. They rejoiced in God's sustaining power.

So Much to Say

As the entourage made its way back to Quito, Don announced he needed "to get it all out of my system." Ted turned on a tape recorder. Don talked through the entire hour-long trip back to Quito. The first of many details tumbled out. . . . *The kidnappers ducked under cover once when a helicopter flew over. Probably a crew from the power company. . . . They kept chainsaws going during the day to make it look like a logging operation. . . . The mountain hideout sat in a misty fog almost continuously. . . . Don saw the sun only a couple of times in two weeks. Always felt chilled.*

When they arrived at a hotel, Ted started trying to get Cheryl on the telephone. The line was busy. Don kept talking to those in the room. Ted dialed again; line still busy. After several attempts, an agent from the U.S. government grabbed the phone and ordered the operator to put the call through.

That's when Cheryl heard a voice interrupting her conversation. "There is an emergency call. Please, hang up immediately." Cheryl quickly complied with the command. When the phone rang a moment later, Cheryl heard Ted's voice on the other end of the line.

"Cheryl, there's a guy here who claims to be your husband, but he doesn't look or smell like the Don Cox I know." Cheryl didn't care what he looked like; she just wanted to hear her husband's voice. Too short, the conversation served only as a down payment for the reunion being arranged for the next day.

Don kept talking after the telephone call. This time the interested parties were representatives from the U.S. Embassy. . . . *The kidnappers were extremely restless the night before the rescue. Up and down the mountain. Very agitated. Didn't go to sleep until probably two o'clock in the morning. They were really tired when the police swooped in. . . . The police found four pistols and a rifle at the mountain hideout. . . . Number 6 whirred the revolving cylinder of a pistol to frighten and torment Don at the platform, while another guard used a rifle to shoot at birds from the clearing. Don thought he might be the next target.*

The debriefing lasted for two-and-a-half hours. Don continued talking even after the officials left.

Neither of two electric shavers would cut Don's whiskers. They had to find a razor. After a refreshing shower, Don put on the clothes Cheryl had placed in the release kit before she left Ecuador. The clothes Don had worn continuously for two weeks were gingerly dropped in the corner of the room. The garbage collector could deal with those smelly garments.

Don and Ted finally crawled into their beds about two in the morning. Don continued talking for quite a while after the lights were turned off.

Cheryl didn't sleep well in Peoria. Too excited.

Don started talking again when the alarm went off at 4:00 A.M. . . . *He had $400 in cash in his pocket the whole time. The kidnappers never checked. He had credit cards too. And keys to every building used by the church. . . . Don knew on December 21 that Ted was involved. That was good.*

At 5:30 Don, Ted, and others from the crisis management team left the hotel for the airport. U.S. Embassy officials and the airlines expedited the check-in procedure. Soon the airplane left Quito headed for Miami. The ultimate destination was Chicago's O'Hare airport.

Don ran right to Cheryl. Their embrace was the kind that mangles eyeglasses.

Cheryl, their sons, and other friends and family members left Peoria about one o'clock. They groaned when they saw that the flight from Miami was delayed. Their wait would last a little bit longer.

The U.S. government officials who traveled on the same flight from Quito to Miami tipped off the airlines as to Don's experience. The kidnappers had considered Don a "product." The airlines treated him with honor. The whole party sat in first class from Miami to Chicago.

The airplane finally pulled into Gate H12 at O'Hare about 5:30 on Christmas afternoon. Since Don sat in the first row of first class, he took off running as soon as the door opened. He surprised everyone by being the first off of the airplane. The pho-

Don and Cheryl embrace at Chicago's O'Hare airport on Christmas Day 1995

tographers on hand to record the event didn't even have their cameras ready.

Don ran right to Cheryl. Their embrace was the kind that mangles eyeglasses. Cheryl had worried about Don having his glasses two weeks before. She didn't even think about it now.

Don hugged each of his sons: Phil, Matt, Paul, Mike. Sometimes tears are easily understood.

Other extended family members crowded in. Don greeted friends and church leaders who had come. The celebration continued at a nearby hotel over dinner. When they paused to thank God for the food, their awareness of God's blessing could not be described in a few words. They could feel in their bones the truth of the child's prayer: God is great; God is good.

Home for Christmas

Don talked through the entire car ride from Chicago to Peoria. So much to say. . . . *When on the mountain, he stood beside the platform to stretch. He tried to exercise regularly. . . . The zipper on the sleeping bag broke. . . . He only lost 10 pounds in the ordeal.*

Don and Cheryl slept only three hours the night of December 25, 1995. Don just kept talking. Cheryl didn't mind, though. Don was home for Christmas.

8

PSALMS OF PROMISE AND PRAISE

The psalmists explored the full range of human emotion, and Cheryl experienced the entire gamut in December 1995. When she could not find words to express the anguish in her heart, the words of a psalm became her prayer. When hope seemed too distant to grasp, a psalm became her anchor. When the joy of a Christmas Day reunion overran her own ability to describe the glory of God's blessing, a psalm began and ended her song of praise.

Many psalms provided comfort and strength to Cheryl, but she kept returning to Psalm 91. Daily she meditated on its truth. Daily she heard God speak a word of comfort to her soul. Daily she found strength to continue the walk of faith.

> He who dwells in the shelter of the Most High
>   will rest in the shadow of the Almighty.
> I will say of the LORD, "He is my refuge and my
>   fortress,
>   my God, in whom I trust."

Surely he will save you from the fowler's snare
and from the deadly pestilence.
He will cover you with his feathers,
and under his wings you will find refuge;
his faithfulness will be your shield and rampart (Psalm 91:1-4).
In retrospect, Psalm 91 helps us see the myriad ways God worked to rescue and protect.

"'Because he loves me,' says the LORD, 'I will rescue him'" (Psalm 91:14a).

No other Nazarene missionary has suffered in quite the same way as Don Cox. Some Nazarene missionaries have endured imprisonment in the midst of war or political unrest. But this was the first time and—by the grace of God—the only time to date that the denomination had faced this type of ordeal.

Law enforcement officials provided greatly needed assistance for the safe resolution of this crisis. The Ecuadorian police unit with expertise in kidnap cases functioned superbly. They quickly identified the false claims of the kidnappers. The U.S. government provided hostage negotiators to serve as advisors. Crisis Consulting International, a Christian organization that counsels mission agencies on security issues, provided an important interface between the church and law enforcement officials.

The crisis management team in Kansas City was initially led by Tim Keeton. Since they could not predict the length of the crisis, the World Mission office began planning for the long term. Dick Sowder became the crisis manager in Kansas City as the second week began.

Mark Graham and Roy Stults assisted with the dissemination of information. Ray Hendrix and José Pacheco prepared transcripts and translations of the telephone calls. Louie Bustle, Jack Stone, and the Board of General Superintendents provided general direction to the process.

David Hayse served as the leader of the crisis management team in Quito. He had helped write the denomination's security plan that included the no-ransom policy. David now faced the difficult task of implementing that policy. Words on paper became a colleague in the rain forest of Ecuador. In addition to negotiators Chuck Howard (Carlos) and Ted Hughes, other members of the crisis management team included Bruno Radi, Dwight Rich, Todd Edgerton, Luis Mesa, and Gustavo Crocker. Each had a specific role in the common effort.

A great partnership developed among people from the various agencies. God used their expertise and cooperation to rescue Don. Those involved on the crisis management teams, however, quickly acknowledge the providential work of God. Statistics reveal that during a rescue attempt, two-thirds of those held hostage die in the action. God spared Don's life.

"I will protect him, for he acknowledges my name" (Psalm 91:14*b*).

God protected Cheryl and the boys while they were still in Ecuador. The kidnappers knew the

Members of the crisis management team with Don in Ecuador:
(l. to r.) **Dwight Rich, Don, Ted Hughes, David Hayse,**
and Todd Edgerton

name of the street but not the address of the Cox's apartment. The outlaw group looked for it unsuccessfully. They watched the seminary campus as well. As the negotiation reached the critical stage, the gang threatened to harm others besides Don. God protected the missionaries, crisis management team, and congregations.

Experts estimate that 70 percent of kidnappings in Latin America are resolved through a ransom payment without police intervention. In Don's case the kidnappers demanded that the police remain uninformed. Even though the special police unit became involved within hours of Don's abduction, the me-

The "Nazarene grapevine" posed another dilemma. A prayer request sometimes morphs into gossip.

dia in Quito did not run the story until after his rescue. Widespread publicity of the case would have had a grave impact on the negotiations. God protected Don by shielding the media from the story.

In the United States a prominent Christian television program asked viewers to pray for Don's release. The crisis management team in Kansas City promptly insisted that the story be withheld from additional broadcasts. No other media outlet picked up the story, greatly relieving everyone concerned for Don's safety.

A Work and Witness team from Arizona happened to be in Ecuador at the time of Don's abduction. They understood the extreme importance of maintaining confidentiality until the crisis passed. The "Nazarene grapevine" posed another dilemma. A prayer request sometimes morphs into gossip, and in this case misinformation could have severe consequences. Just as God protected Daniel by shutting the mouths of the lions, so God protected Don through restrained, disciplined conversations.

"He will call upon me, and I will answer him" (Psalm 91:15a).

People did not hold back, however, in talking to God on Don's behalf. Thousands of people around the world offered prayers for God's intervention on a mountainside in Ecuador. Hundreds of congregations prayed for Don's safe release. The biweekly Prayer Mobilization Line distributed by Nazarene Missions International, under Nina Gunter's leadership, called intercessors to attention. A mighty army went to battle on their knees.

Don and Cheryl's son Paul was a student at Olivet Nazarene University (ONU) when Don was abducted. Cheryl contacted Brian and Joan Wilson, then missionaries on home assignment living in the ONU missionary residence. Paul knew the Wilsons since they were part of the missionary family in Ecuador. After Cheryl called, Joan went to see Paul. Joan also informed leaders in the ONU community. The students initiated a prayer meeting, surrounding their fellow student with petitions of faith.

Don prayed alone on the mountainside. He prayed for his release, of course, but Don's primary concern was that the kidnappers not harm his family. God heard Don's prayer.

Cheryl discovered Psalm 140 as God's message for her on December 21. One of her good friends called that day, excited about what she found in the Bible, a passage seemingly written just for Don. The two women rejoiced that God had directed both of them to the same chapter in the Bible on the same day. Psalm 140 became their common prayer.

Do not grant the wicked their desires, O LORD;
do not let their plans succeed (Psalm 140:8a).
God answered their prayer.

A friend of Don and Cheryl awoke in the middle of the night with an intense sense that she must pray for Don that instant. She never felt the same urgency before or after that moment. When Don returned home, they discovered that this friend prayed for him at the time the special police unit moved up the mountain to rescue Don.

The boys had "angels" near them too.

Many pastors included Don in their pastoral prayer during the morning worship service on December 24, 1995. In the midst of that prayer time, one pastor felt God remove the burden from him. He began to thank God for answering the prayers of people around the world. Three hours later a telephone call confirmed what God had already revealed.

"I will be with him in trouble" (Psalm 91:15*b*).

God stood near Cheryl in the form of friends, colleagues, and family. The authorities wanted life to appear normal around the apartment in Quito so as not to provide help to the kidnappers. As a result, some friends were discouraged from stopping by for a visit. Cheryl never lacked for a companion, however, as she had someone with her the whole week. Many provided food; others assisted with household chores.

The boys had "angels" near them too. A couple of teachers came alongside Matt, Mike, and Phil to support and encourage. For security reasons the boys were picked up at the front door of the apartment and entered their school through a back gate. They completed final exams the week after Don's abduction.

The decision to leave Ecuador proved difficult for the boys. Mike and Matt would graduate with top honors in just five months. They did not want to relinquish what they had worked so hard to achieve. Besides, Ecuador was home for them; the United States, a foreign country. Mike verbalized the struggle the boys went through in a poem written for a school assignment three months after Don's rescue. He wrote in the style of a psalm:

But I beg humbly on my knees to allow me to
    return to my homeland.
The land calls me to return, yet I hear not from
    you.

In the end God's presence quieted the laments.

Omar told Don on December 21 that Ted served as the negotiator. This news encouraged Don, something Ted hoped would happen when he decided to use his real name. During their conversation on December 22, Omar told Ted that Don was "trusting in you an awful lot, and he sends his regards, and he hopes to see you very soon." Later in the same conversation Omar said that Don was "very happy and calm because you (Ted) are handling this." Even though Ted could not physically be with Don, simply knowing about his participation in the negotiations brought Don comfort. Ted realized that he had little to offer without God's presence. He depended totally on the Lord to help him think quickly and speak prudently.

From the beginning of this ordeal, personnel at the International Headquarters expressed their concern for the extended Cox family. Retired mission-

Don and Ted at a hotel following the rescue

ary Charles Gates accepted the call to serve as a pastor to the family members in the United States. He called various ones every day, providing updated information on the negotiations and praying with them. Louie Bustle and the general superintendents had regular contact with the family as well.

Once Cheryl returned to the United States, calls started coming in from all over the country. People they had met on Work and Witness teams or at deputation services called Cheryl to share words of comfort. The telephone rang often, each conversation a source of strength.

When it became evident that the Cox family could not return to Ecuador for security reasons, they scrambled to make plans for the unexpected home assignment. A member of the church in Peoria had a furnished house available while waiting for an estate to settle. The Coxes moved in, paying only the expenses. They found a Christian school for the boys with the tuition paid by an anonymous donor. God provided everything they needed, an unmistakable sign of divine presence.

"I will deliver him and honor him" (Psalm 91:15c).

Understandably, congregations began asking Don to come and tell the story of God's sustaining grace. Just three days after his rescue, the first service took place in Don and Cheryl's home church in Peoria.

A few weeks later while in Florida for a speaking engagement, Don slept alone in a bedroom for the first time since his return to the United States. He awoke terrified, shaking uncontrollably. Don turned on a light to get his bearings and read for a while. Sleep came soon, and he had a restful night. God continued to deliver Don, even after his return to the States.

After that flashback Don and Cheryl spent a weekend with a specialist in Virginia. She listened to their story and asked probing questions before making recommendations on how they might bring closure to the traumatic experiences. She recommended that they meet regularly with a counselor in Chicago to continue the healing process, something Don, Cheryl, and the boys all did.

The Lord has continued to bring deliverance to Ted as well. He relived parts of his experience as the one responsible to talk with the abductors. Hostage negotiators with an emotional attachment to the kidnap victim tend to have a more difficult time finding closure than a detached negotiator. Ted has no regrets about working for his friend's release, but his role was not without its emotional challenges. The Lord has been faithful.

The United States government presented Ted with a citation in recognition of his excellent service as the negotiator in this crisis. The United States Air Force asked both Ted and Don to participate in a debriefing in an effort to improve the training for pilots who could be caught in a hostage situation.

The Cox family on December 31, 1995:
(L. to r.) **Paul, Phil, Mike, Cheryl, Matt, and Don**

"With long life will I satisfy him and show him my salvation" (Psalm 91:16).

One month after the rescue, Cheryl returned to Quito to pack the family's belongings. They would not return to Ecuador as missionaries but would be reassigned after an eight-month furlough. The family attended Mike and Matt's high school graduation in Quito in May 1996. The school in Ecuador accepted the credits from the school in Illinois so that they graduated with high honors. The boys were baptized during that trip too. All four of the Cox boys have since graduated from college.

Don and Cheryl continue to serve the Lord faithfully. At first they went to Guatemala; then they moved to Mexico. As of this writing, they work in the JESUS Film Harvest Partners office in Olathe, Kansas. Don continues to use his aptitude for numbers as the financial controller, and Cheryl serves as the database manager. The kidnapping incident brought a degree of notoriety to Don, but it hasn't changed his approach to life. He faithfully served the Lord before the abduction, most often behind the scenes. He has faithfully served the Lord since his rescue.

Don's rock-solid assurance of eternal life held him steady during the two-week storm.

Don would be the first to tell you that there was nothing heroic about him during the kidnapping. He vomited when the abduction took place. Anxiety caused him to suffer with diarrhea throughout the ordeal. Don had little confidence in his survival. He thought the kidnappers would eventually kill him but desperately hoped he would not be tortured.

Don's rock-solid assurance of eternal life held him steady during the two-week storm. The thugs might snuff out his physical life, but as a man redeemed by the blood of Jesus, he would live forever with his Lord and Savior.

Just before he climbed into the sleeping bag and positioned the blankets on his last night on the Andean mountain, Don read 1 Corinthians 3. The phrase from verse 23, "You belong to Christ" (NASB), echoed in his thoughts like the reverberation in a rocky canyon. "Don Cox, you belong to Christ."

Don rested that night in the promise of eternal life because he belonged to Christ. He awoke to shouts at sunrise and the glory of liberation.

> The LORD lives! Praise be to my Rock!
>> Exalted be God my Savior! . . .
> You exalted me above my foes;
>> from violent men you rescued me.
> Therefore I will praise you among the nations,
>> O LORD;
>> I will sing praises to your name (Psalm 18:46, 48b-49).

CALL TO ACTION

After reading this book, please consider doing one or more of the following:

1. Pray daily for the safety of Nazarene missionaries who often serve in areas hostile to the gospel. Especially remember those missionaries who are ministering underground in creative access areas.

2. Pray for those who are viewed as "enemies" of Christianity. Jesus said, "Love your enemies and pray for those who persecute you" (Matt. 5:44b).

3. Write a note of encouragement to Don and Cheryl Cox. Send to JESUS Film Harvest Partners, 720 S. Rogers Rd., Suite A, Olathe, KS 66202.

4. Help promote the International Day of Prayer (IDOP) in your church. See Web site below.

5. Become more informed about persecuted Christians around the world. Information about the "persecuted church" can be found at the following Web sites:
   - IDOP for the Persecuted Church <www.persecuted church.org>
   - The Voice of the Martyrs <www.persecution.com>
   - Christian Solidarity Worldwide <www.cswusa.com>
   - International Christian Concern <www.persecution .org>
   - Jubilee Campaign <www.jubileecampaign.org>
   - Open Doors with Brother Andrew <www.open doorsusa.org>
   - World Evangelical Alliance <www.worldevangelical .org>

Wes Eby, editor

PRONUNCIATION GUIDE

The following information will assist in pronouncing some unfamiliar words in this book. The suggested pronunciations, though not always precise, are close approximations of the way the terms are pronounced.

Calderon	kahl-deh-ROHN
Carcelén	kahr-say-LAYN
colocasia	koh-loh-KAY-shuh
Crocker, Gustavo	KRAH-ker goos-TAH-voh
Ecuador	eh-kwah-DOHR
Guadalajara	GWAH-dah-lah-HAH-rah
Guayaquil	gwie-ah-KEEL
Los Bancos	lohs BAHN-kohs
Mesa, Luis	MAY-sah loo-EES
Pacheco, José	pah-CHEH-koh hoh-SAY
primos	PREE-mohs
Pusey	PYOO-see
Quito	KEE-toh
Radi, Liliana	RA-dee lih-lee-AH-nah
Seminario Teologico Nazareno	sehm-ih-NAH-ree-oh tay-oh-LOH-hee-koh nah-zah-RAY-noh
Veigl	VIE-guhl